We

GW01425226

The idea of 'no

One is that of t.._ ...g..p...i. or the day to which the activity of morning leads; the other is the time when the sun is at the top of the sky, the heat at its most intense, and when, in many cultures, the custom is to take a midday rest—or at least a long lunch!

Both these images are explored here: 'seizing the day' and also pausing for breath, taking stock and not allowing ourselves to be driven without rest. For a number of years, Stephen Rand helped to lead a church called Kairos, a word used in the Bible to pinpoint a significant time, the moment to act before the opportunity is lost. In our opening article he unpacks the importance of this principle for our walk as Christian disciples, balanced by the Spirit's guidance as we seek to understand God's calling.

As the world has become busier and more pressurized, awareness has grown of the benefits of living according to a different rhythm. For this 'Noon' issue, Henry Wansbrough, a Benedictine monk of Ampleforth Abbey, has written a profile of St Benedict and the framework for work, rest and prayer that he devised soon after the fall of the Roman Empire, which still orders the lives of many today.

We also have Sarah Parry sharing how her inner-city church was transformed from near dereliction into a bustling centre for the local community. Amy Boucher Pye, meanwhile, describes the challenge of parenting young children and finding God in a small oasis of peace, in the middle of a transatlantic flight.

Work and rest, busyness and stillness—may you enjoy both as you read *Quiet Spaces* over the coming days.

NAOMI STARKEY

Naomi Starkey

1

This compilation copyright © BRF 2008
Authors retain copyright in their own work
Illustrations copyright © Ian Mitchell, Ray and Corinne Burrows, 2008

Published by
The Bible Reading Fellowship
15 The Chambers, Vineyard
Abingdon OX14 3FE
United Kingdom
Tel: +44 (0)1865 319700
Email: enquiries@brf.org.uk
Websites: www.brf.org.uk and www.quietspaces.org.uk

ISBN 978 1 84101 541 5
First published 2008
10 9 8 7 6 5 4 3 2 1 0
All rights reserved

Acknowledgments
Scripture quotations taken from the Holy Bible, Today's New International Version, copyright
© 2004 by International Bible Society, are used by permission of Hodder & Stoughton Publishers,
a division of Hodder Headline Ltd. All rights reserved. 'TNIV' is a registered trademark of
International Bible Society.

Scripture quotations taken from the Holy Bible, New International Version, copyright © 1973, 1978,
1984, 1995 by International Bible Society, are used by permission of Hodder & Stoughton Publishers,
a division of Hodder Headline Ltd. All rights reserved. 'NIV' is a registered trademark of International
Bible Society. UK trademark number 1448790.

Scripture quotations taken from The New Revised Standard Version of the Bible, Anglicized Edition,
copyright © 1989, 1995 by the Division of Christian Education of the National Council of the
Churches of Christ in the USA, are used by permission. All rights reserved.

Scripture quotations taken from the Contemporary English Version of the Bible published by
HarperCollins Publishers, copyright © 1991, 1992, 1995 American Bible Society.

'And that will be heaven' by Evangeline Paterson, reproduced by permission of Carolyn Rowland-Jones.

A catalogue record for this book is available from the British Library

Printed by Gutenberg Press, Tarxien, Malta

Quiet Spaces

VOLUME 11

CONTENTS

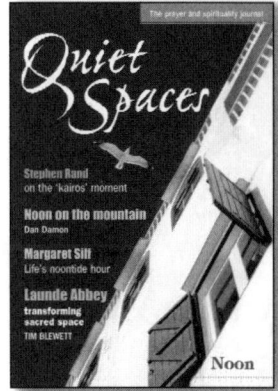

High Noon

the secret is in the timing

Stephen Rand is the co-chair of Jubilee Debt Campaign and the author of 'When the Time Was Right' (BRF, 2006).

Gary Cooper is the town marshal. Today he gets married and ceases to be a lawman: he is starting a new life. He is due to leave town with his bride—then he hears that a man he sent to prison is on his way to town with revenge on his thoughts. His train will arrive at noon.

Gary's bride and his friends tell him to leave. No one will back him when he decides to stay and face the challenge. So as the train comes closer, Gary is all alone.

And do you know? I can't remember for the life of me what happens. My memory of the film is only of the building pressure as the clock ticks remorselessly on, getting closer and closer to High Noon, the moment of truth. It may be in black and white, but the suspense is all too real, and it is marked by the clock.

But then, two thousand years ago, there was a factual moment of truth that came at noon. 'It was now about noon, and darkness came over the whole land until three in the afternoon, for the sun stopped shining. And the curtain of the temple was torn in two. Jesus called out with a loud voice, "Father, into your hands I commit my spirit." When he had said this, he breathed his last' (Luke 23:44–46, TNIV).

Matthew, Mark, Luke—each one tells his readers the exact time when the cosmos refused to look on the awful scene of the death of the Son of God. Luke is the one who tells us that it was also the moment when the way to God was opened up to all— no more fear of the presence of God, no more priest to act on our behalf. Now the curtain, the way in to the presence of God, was torn open and light flooded into the abnormal darkness.

We are told that the secret of great comedy is timing. The apostle Paul is certain that this piece of timing was no joke. It was the fulcrum of time, no random event or tragic accident: 'You see, at just the right time, when we were still powerless, Christ died for the ungodly' (Romans 5:6). He was just as certain about the incarnation: 'When the time was right, God sent his Son, and a woman gave birth to him' (Galatians 4:4, CEV).

For God, who is not bound by time but is the creator of time, the one who set the earth in motion with the sun to rule the day and the moon the night, the clock was ticking round to the greatest divine appointment of all. Generation after generation, God's people had waited. Now the time had come.

I spent some years helping to lead a church called Kairos. It was started by someone who wanted to have a church full of contemporary relevance—and he chose to call it by a Greek word that very few people have ever heard of. *Kairos* is a word meaning 'time', and is often used in the Bible for a significant time, the moment of a new start, a new direction, because 'the time has come'. So the name of the church was intended to reflect this sense of 'now' being the moment, the right time.

… the clock was ticking round to the greatest divine appointment of all

---

The ancient Greeks described Kairos as the god of the 'fleeting moment', 'a favourable opportunity'. He was depicted with a tuft of hair on his forehead, so that there was something to grab, to 'seize the day'. But the back of his head was bald: once the moment has passed, there is nothing to hold on to; the special time cannot be regained.

A famous statue of Kairos carried an epigram by the poet Poseidippos carved on its base:

... the successful farmer is the one who harvests at just the right time

Who are you? *Time who subdues all things.*
Why do you stand on tiptoe? *I am ever running.*
And why do you have a pair of wings on your feet? *I fly with the wind.*
And why do you hold a razor in your right hand? *As a sign that I am sharper than any sharp edge.*
And why does your hair hang over your face? *For him who meets me to take me by the forelock.*
And why, in heaven's name, is the back of your head bald? *Because none whom I have once raced by on my winged feet will now, though he wishes it sore, take hold of me from behind.*

Why did the artist fashion you? *For your sake, stranger, and he set me up in the porch as a lesson.*

This is the great truth of time, God's timing. On the one hand, it is full of glorious opportunity: a *kairos* moment is world-changing. But if we miss it, what an opportunity missed! As a great cricket watcher, I know the feeling: it is when the batsman hits the ball steepling into the air and the fielder gets into position underneath and waits for it to come down—and the whole match could depend on whether he can hold the catch or whether he will drop it.

Paul was on a missionary journey, sharing the good news of Jesus, when he was arrested and brought before Felix, the Roman governor (whose name, perhaps ironically, is the Latin word meaning 'happiness'). Felix listens to Paul—and then he misses the moment: 'As Paul talked about righteousness, self-control and the judgment to come, Felix was afraid and said, "That's enough for now! You may leave. When I find it convenient, I will send for you"' (Acts 24:25, TNIV). And guess what? That convenient time never arrived. He missed the moment. Perhaps Paul was thinking of Felix when he wrote, 'I tell you, now is the time of God's favour, now is the day of salvation' (2 Corinthians 6:2).

Jesus used the word *kairos* to refer to harvest (see, for example, Matthew 13:30). Now I am to plants and farming what Homer Simpson is to quantum physics, but I know that the successful farmer is the one who harvests at just the right time, when the crop has ripened but before it can be ruined by bad weather.

Getting the moment right is sometimes a bigger challenge than we think. We've all regretted a missed opportunity to say a helpful or encouraging word; we've all dithered, hesitant to take the risk, and seen the moment pass. But there have been those great moments when we got it right—and a relationship was mended, a new direction was taken, a chain of events was set in motion that brought a harvest of its own.

As I write this piece, I am planning a great event to mark a significant anniversary: in May 1998, 70,000 people from across Britain and the world formed a human chain in Birmingham to demand debt cancellation for the world's poorest nations from the G8, the leaders of the world's richest nations. It was a seminal event, a milestone on the journey to justice.

So, on Sunday 18 May 2008, people will once again gather in Birmingham. Ten years on, billions of dollars of debt have been cancelled; the lives of millions have been changed. And even though there is still more to be done—injustice, exploitation and imbalances of power still characterize relationships between rich and poor nations—it is right to recognize that world-changing day ten years ago, when the Jubilee trumpet was heard.

I was involved back then because one woman heard the voice of God, came to me when I was working at Tearfund, and urged me to take the unique opportunity offered by the approaching millennium to focus on a new start for the world's poorest nations. She could see that the time was right.

Getting the moment right is sometimes a bigger challenge than we think

So could those who started Tearfund, way back in 1968. As the children of Biafra brought the faces of starvation to our TV screens for the first time, Morgan Derham, the General Secretary of the Evangelical Alliance, urged his board to seize the opportunity, and George Hoffman was appointed to take The Evangelical Alliance Relief Fund forward.

The time was right. Evangelical Christians had lost their inheritance of life-enhancing, world-changing action bequeathed by Wilberforce, Shaftesbury and so many other pioneering men and women. But as

George Hoffman travelled the country, preached in churches and wrote articles, so the simple words of the Bible became expressed through a charity that helped to change the face of the church and bring new life and hope to hundreds of thousands of needy people across the globe. 'This is how we know what love is: Jesus Christ laid down his life for us. And we ought to lay down our lives for one another. If any one of you has material possessions and sees a

How do we know when it is a moment to wait or a moment to act?

This understanding of time is characterized by **openness to the future**

brother or sister in need but has no pity on them, how can the love of God be in you?' (1 John 3:16–17).

You could add in some of the great *kairos* moments of world history. I can still recall staying up to watch a man walk on the moon for the first time; but then I'm old enough to remember what I was doing when I heard that President John F. Kennedy had been shot. I saw Nelson Mandela walking out of a South African jail and the crowds tearing down the Berlin Wall.

These great turning points depended on human beings making the right decisions at the right time. That's why I am so aware of the need to be discerning. Timing is not only the secret of great comedy; it is the secret of living life the way God wants us to live.

How do we know when it is a moment to wait or a moment to act?

Jesus was scathing in his denunciation of the religious leaders of his day: 'Hypocrites! You know how to interpret the appearance of the earth and the sky. How is it that you don't know how to interpret this present time?' (Luke 12:56).

Interpretation is a gift of God's Spirit. We need the help of the Holy Spirit to understand what is happening in our culture as a church; we need that same help to know how to respond to our own changing circumstances and the specific opportunities that arrive each day. In the words of Ephesians, 'Be very careful, then, how you live—not as unwise but as wise, making the most of every opportunity, because the days are evil. Therefore do not be foolish, but understand what the Lord's will is. Do not get drunk on wine, which leads to debauchery. Instead, be filled with the Spirit' (5:15–18).

For the apostle Paul, his whole travelling life had to be governed by

A surviving section of the Berlin Wall, symbol of a great *kairos* moment in history

the prompting of God's Spirit— when to move, when to stay put. He could see the link between being filled with the Spirit and being able to make the most of every opportunity.

Not long after my wife and I had become part of the leadership team at Kairos, we all met together one Sunday afternoon to pray and reflect on where we felt God was directing us as a church. We went to a retreat centre not far away and, by one of those strange coincidences that we feel might mean a little more than first appears, it too was called Kairos. In the entrance hall there was a little plaque, which said, '*Kairos*— a Greek word meaning the favourable time or graced moment. This understanding of time is characterized by openness to the future. Now is the favourable time and Christ is its turning point. *Kairos* encourages us to be patient so we can let go and let God.'

The clock is ticking. Your high noon may be approaching. Seize the day. ■

© Louise Blackmore

More than fixing the roof

Sarah Parry is minister of Shoreditch Tabernacle Baptist Church in Tower Hamlets. She has been a minister for 15 years and has a particular interest in the use of church buildings in inner cities.

There was a door at the end of the corridor in this sprawling church building, but getting to it wasn't going to be easy. Much later, obstacles overcome, the caretaker and I forced the door open to find a sunless room filled with… well, what was it filled with? Strange piles that looked suspiciously like a massive heap of old shoes, a collection of doors and rotting Victorian exercise equipment. The parquet floor had been ripped up at some point and the window boarded in. Everything was dirty, untouched and useless. The room next door also had its window boarded over, even though, worryingly, it was in use as a Sunday school room.

It had been a long morning viewing the premises of Shoreditch Tabernacle, both the 1960s church and the Victorian church school. Exhausted, filthy and depressed, I wondered how the church had kept going all these years, never turning anything out in a building that was deteriorating with every passing year. What I needed was a long hot bath; what the church might need was a whole lot more complicated.

Shoreditch Tabernacle Church and its mission school lie in the heart of East London. Bordering Spitalfields to the south and Bethnal Green to the east, their past is woven together with the social history of the area. Most significantly, Shoreditch lies outside the city wall, historically where the dispossessed and dissenters lived. It's the place where the earliest theatres opened and where immigrant communities set up homes and businesses.

In the 19th century, the square mile of Shoreditch alone contained more than 300 licensed public houses servicing the notorious Nichol Street and Hoxton slums. The Tab, meanwhile, educated children, supported women and ran clubs for men, and propounded fresh air and exercise for all, not only preaching good news but addressing the harshest consequences of poverty and deprivation.

By the mid-20th century, significant changes were affecting the church. In World War II, an incendiary bomb set fire to the roof of the main lecture hall. The church sanctuary did not take a direct hit but a bomb exploding nearby in Calvert Avenue damaged the church, making it unsafe and impossible to rescue. After the war it was demolished and the current 1960s building replaced it, but the resources poured into the new church meant that the church school was neglected and the leaking roof unattended. Meanwhile, the great eastern emigration began. As slums were cleared, people moved out, mostly further east to Leyton and Romford, leaving the congregation decimated.

In 2001, around the time I began my ministry at

> Exhausted, filthy and depressed, I wondered how the church had kept going all these years

the Tab, some people were asking whether there was anything left worth saving. I had questions too. What on earth was I doing here? Would my ministry see the final burial of this church? I knew from the way colleagues questioned me curiously about Shoreditch that they believed I was making a foolish mistake in leaving leafy Hertfordshire for inner-city Tower Hamlets. I knew from the regional minister that not many ministers—none of sane mind—would be interested in Shoreditch Tab. I knew from my own uncertainty that I thought they were right. Nevertheless, here we were: one minister, one husband and one basset hound, apparently ready for anything.

If Shoreditch Tabernacle was to survive, one thing was certain: it needed hope, a vision for the future where things might not only be bearable but positively good. Inseparable from the vision was the necessity to make decisions and follow them through. What could this small multicultural congregation do, burdened with semi-derelict buildings and no money in the bank account?

Should they accept that the lifespan of the Shoreditch Tab had come to an end? There was no dishonour in that. Was it time to consolidate, sell the old school for cash and invest for the future? That was the low-risk option. Was it time to reverse the culture of neglect and reimagine the church's mission purpose for 21st-century Shoreditch? This was the courageous option that the church took.

One thing that inspired me about the church community was that they dared to hope that this church and community site could be resurrected. They were also prepared, in theory at any rate, to work and pray together. The restoration of the buildings became a symbol of the restorative aims that the people in the building owned for themselves and their community. In short, they dared to have faith.

Jesus at Nazareth speaks of hope: his vision is to

> **Would my ministry see the final burial of this church?**

'bring good news to the poor… release to the captives… sight to the blind, to let the oppressed go free' (see Luke 4:18, NRSV). These words powerfully articulate the transformation of communities in the kingdom of God. Jesus' reading comes from Isaiah, and in Isaiah, rather than in Luke, it goes on to say, 'They shall build up the ancient ruins, they shall raise up the former devastations; they shall repair the ruined cities, the devastations of many generations' (Isaiah 61:4).

Who are 'they' who are going to do all this building? They are the blind, the poor and the captives who have experienced God's liberation. They are the builders—the once broken people. To those of us at the Tab who felt inadequate for the task, this was enormously encouraging. For those of us who felt uncomfortable with the risks taken and the daily uncertainty of the future, it was a comfort.

One restoration project is usually enough for any one group or individual. Living on a rollercoaster, which is what it felt like for several years, is not always exhilarating. There were some appalling times tossed in with the wonderful moments. Early on, I despaired as the first of a long line of skips was filled with clutter on Saturday by one half of the congregation, only to be faithfully emptied and the clutter returned to church on Sunday by the other half. Change comes slowly. Persistence is valuable.

Contrast this with the delight and prayers of thankfulness when our Heritage Lottery grant was funded, or extraordinary meetings with architects and site managers when the impossible became improbably achievable. I can identify with the disciples in the stormy seas yelling at Jesus to wake up and do something, and being amazed at what happened when he did.

Today, Shoreditch Tabernacle and the Tab Centre are places of transformation. Opened in 2005, the Tab Centre is situated in a now stunningly beautiful building which runs or partners with a diversity of projects to address poverty and deprivation and

There were some appalling times tossed in with the wonderful moments

One restoration project is usually enough

> ... a diversity of projects to address poverty and deprivation and **celebrate life and living**

celebrate life and living. We have spent nearly £2million and the church is debt-free. The founding principles of the transformed school have been kept but are innovatively reinterpreted for modern-day Shoreditch.

Members of the spirituality group relax in the reception lounge and consider the pros and cons of installing a TV to add to their comfort. Volunteers in the kitchen have adapted to the high-tech equipment while I'm still working out how to make coffee. People stream through the halls and rooms; whoever comes in is welcomed, whether they are sex workers or film stars. Things are not trouble-free but we try to keep in mind the story Jesus told of the banquet to which all are invited, especially those who are not used to being welcomed.

One of our most successful projects is with women prisoners as they are transitioning through imprisonment to release after long sentences. Coming out of prison can be a lonely and depressing experience, leaving women emotionally vulnerable and likely to reoffend. Typically these women have experienced poverty and exploitation, which affects them and their children, perpetuating cycles of abuse and crime. We are able to help a small number with volunteering and paid work, providing support for them and their families over several years.

Just recently, one of the women told me she had passed her first accounting exam and has a new job in the finance team of a national charity. She told me how much difference the support of people at the Tab had made to her life. We laughed and danced for joy.

As we talked in the sunlight, I realized we were in the same room that I had first seen in darkness, piled high with discarded shoes and unwanted doors. It had been a place of despair. How could this possibly be the same room? It was as though resurrection had entered the fabric of the walls, leapt into our joined hands and shared our laughter. ∎

Noon on the
mountain

Dan Damon presents the weekly 'Reporting Religion' and the daily news programme 'World Update' on the BBC World Service.

No one needs to climb a mountain, even a little one, to find faith...

I found my faith on a mountain. OK, you might be thinking, a pilgrimage to a holy mountain—a lot of people do that to strengthen their faith; it's nothing unusual.

I hadn't gone up there on a pilgrimage, though, and I certainly wasn't looking for a religious revelation. I went to make a film about some remarkable Bosnian friends who had decided to use the opportunity of a brief lull in the fighting in 1994 not to go to the beach or seek asylum in the West but to climb an 8000m Himalayan peak in Pakistan.

In among the rockfalls and landslides and bursting rivers and oxygen deprivation and days of hard walking, God showed me what faith could do and told me to go looking for it when I got down from the mountain again.

No one needs to climb a mountain, even a little one, to find faith, but people of faith do often go looking for God up there. For many believers around the world, God is remote and impossibly high in the sky. Not surprising, then, that mountains feature in so many scriptures and rituals. On a mountain, it seems like you might get a bit closer to the Creator. Maybe the massiveness of the mountain and the dizzying distance from the summit to the far horizon offer a glimpse of the vastness of his creation.

Buddhists long to walk around the 6000m-high Kangrin Poche in Tibet. They believe that ten circuits round the mountain in a lifetime will save a pilgrim from going through the sufferings of hell before embarking on a new life. Shinto followers in Japan worship the mountains themselves and the spirits they feel within them.

Christians have holy mountains, of course—Mount Athos and the other mountain monasteries in Greece and Mount Sinai in Egypt, where pilgrims climb in the dark to watch the dawn.

Christians, though, have the

> **On a mountain, it seems like you might get a bit closer to the Creator**

comfort of knowing that God doesn't live only on the top of the mountain. He came down to live in the dust like us and to sweat in the heat of the valley. He died there, came back to life again, and stayed in the person of the Holy Spirit—to kneel beside us when we pray, to walk with us through each day and, if we're listening, to shout at us when we're heading off in the wrong direction.

Down on the plains, I had been wandering aimlessly and behaving badly. I didn't believe that for a moment, of course. I had found an exciting career as a reporter and cameraman and had scored some successes, even some exclusives,

covering the wars and revolutions of Eastern Europe and the Middle East. I thought I was remarkable, maybe even immortal. I'd come through a lot of shooting and shelling, after all. And if you work in war zones there are no rules any more, except to do what is necessary for survival, so who needs discipline and self-denial?

I'd befriended a special police unit in Sarajevo, Bosnia's capital. They were hard-drinking heroes who went into action with rifles against tanks. In the first days of the war, they had probably saved the city from being overrun by the Serb army. Before the conflict began in 1991, they had all been members of the Bosnian Mountaineering Club. As the front lines hardened and they sat in their trenches through the three harsh winters of '91, '92 and '93, they kept their spirits up by planning an expedition. It had to be special, the best a climber could imagine: why not the Himalayas?

Did they ever believe it would happen? I doubt it, but it was a brave dream for brave men—and when the chance came, I suppose they didn't know how to stop themselves. For a few months at the start of 1994, the UN managed to impose some kind of ceasefire and, for certain purposes and with a special permit, some lucky Sarajevans could get to the airport and fly out. A Bosnian attempt on the Himalayas became one of those special reasons, so my friends invited me to film them fulfilling their destiny.

© Galyna Andrushko, Used under licence from Shutterstock, Inc.

I didn't hear God himself at first, only his evangelists. All of them were Muslims.

The people in that part of Pakistan are Shi'ites, who believe that Mohammed's rightful successor, Hussein, was unlawfully deprived of his inheritance and killed in a battle at Karbala, now in Iraq. But a saviour is coming, the 12th Imam, who is hiding somewhere on earth and will reveal himself when humankind has reached the lowest point of corruption and desecration.

Shia Islam is a religion of waiting and suffering. As a minority in the Islamic world, Shi'ites have often been persecuted by the Sunni majority (descendants of the victors at Karbala) and they have learnt to bear the utmost hardship. In some of their rituals, they inflict wounds on themselves to demonstrate their commitment to suffering.

The porters and drivers for the Bosnian attempt on the Himalayas were Shi'ites living in one of the harshest places where anyone has built a home. Their villages are remote from any form of state provision—no electricity, no doctors, only the Pakistani army's helicopters flying overhead to supply the garrisons on the disputed Kashmiri border with India. They can scrape some small fields clear of stones high among the rocks and grow some food. Most of all, they can earn money as porters to the trekkers and climbers making a nine-day journey to the Pakistani side

This is a story about the personal summit I crested, my path to faith

What happened to the expedition is a great tale for another time. I'd love to tell you what it's like swinging in a basket across a raging torrent— but not now. This is a story about the personal summit I crested, my path to faith.

of the Himalayan range, where K2 and some other 8000m peaks draw Western adventurers during the short summer months.

What made our party especially interesting to these devout mountain people was that we came from a country, Bosnia, where they knew that Muslims were fighting Christians. Wasn't that what the imams in the mosques had told them: Orthodox Serbs were killing Bosnian Muslims? Some of them had even seen pictures of it on the television when they went down to the valleys. So we Western-looking mountaineers must be good Muslims.

How shocked they were, then, to discover that we could not pray— just didn't know the words. We couldn't even begin to explain that not all of us were Muslims. Apart from me, two of the party were Serb and one was a Croat, and therefore a Catholic; soldiers who, like many others, had fought alongside Bosnian Muslims in opposition to the illegal and deadly nationalistic war for ethnic purity launched by Slobodan Milosevic in 1991.

We didn't tell them, either, that stashed among the ropes, crampons and dried food for the expedition were a couple of bottles of single malt whisky to be opened in celebration at the end of the climb. To our porters, it was bad enough that we couldn't pray—the news that Bosnian Muslims like a drink and distil some of the best grape brandy

in the world would have brought down lightning bolts of divine retribution. We were, quite evidently, a group of lost souls who needed to be brought back to the true faith.

Perhaps we could be forgiven. They knew, too, from the imams at the mosque about the evils of communism—how the Russian atheists, allies of India, had blown up mosques in Central Asia and the

> How shocked they were,
> then, to discover that we
> could not pray—
> **just didn't know the words**

Caucasus, or turned them into museums, and then tried to occupy the Muslim lands of Afghanistan. Yugoslavia was communist, too, wasn't it?

They weren't far wrong, really. When the founder of Socialist Federal Yugoslavia, Marshal Tito, decreed that 'Muslim' should be a nationality in the Republic of Bosnia to balance the influence of Serbs and Croats, 'Muslim Atheist' became an official term on the registration documents of thousands of Yugoslavia's citizens.

So as we drove for a day in rickety jeeps and then walked for eight days more up the mountain and across the glacier, our porters took it on themselves to rehearse us in the

They were happier still because they had found a way to **share that faith by teaching us**

ancient Arabic words of the rituals that would save us from hell.

I was captivated and enthralled. These were some of the poorest people I had ever met, walking up steep mountain paths and through rivers, carrying huge loads, wearing flip-flops, for a couple of dollars a day—and they were happy because they had a strong faith. They were happier still because they had found a way to share that faith by teaching us.

I learned those prayers as well as I could: I can remember most of them still. I thought about this miracle of faith in hard places as I walked for hours through the heat of the day (even snowy mountains are hot in daytime in summer in those latitudes).

Should I, then, become a Muslim, if Islam was so powerful? I should at least find out more about it when I got home.

I read the Quran; I read the study guides. I learned a lot about God. But after just a few weeks of study, I realized that the words seemed remote. I had no relationship with that tradition, however inspiring its moral principles. I was learning about God but not hearing him.

It didn't take me long after that to find the tradition that did speak to me and brought God's voice alive. As I read again the Bible of my youth, but this time in the light of the powerful faith and prayer I had found on the mountain, Jesus told me to spend the rest of my life seeking to understand his words in the Gospels and to honour the ancient books of the Old Testament from which he had learnt.

My story doesn't mean that I think all faiths are equally valid paths towards God, but finding God through learning to pray on the mountain with those Shia Muslim porters has made me a friend of Islam. In a changing world, I believe that's why God met me there, all those thousands of metres high.

I'm sad that some Muslims don't want to be friends with me—and I get depressed and sometimes angry when, in the name of Islam, a few who call themselves faithful refuse to share the love of God as a starting point for peace. ∎

Finding God's rest

in the parenting years

Amy Boucher Pye
is an American
who has lived in
the UK for the past
ten years. She
works in Christian
publishing and
has written for such periodicals as
'The Church Times', 'The Church of
England Newspaper', 'Woman Alive'
and 'Christian Marketplace'. She
makes her home in north London
with her husband and young family.

... to become a living sacrifice

'Is that your carry-on item?' the man at the check-in counter demanded.

My heart sank. I had duly measured it at home and, knowing it was an inch over if the wheels were included, hoped it would be OK. 'Yes. Is that a problem?'

'We'll need to measure it. And what's this other bag?' he asked, equally insistent.

'That,' I said through gritted teeth, 'is my diaper bag and it's *allowed*.'

But the first bag wasn't—even though it had been on previous trips. So in the full view of the bemused travellers queuing behind me, I unpacked the case of the necessary bits to keep a four-year-old and a four-month-old fed and clean for a nine-hour flight, shoved the stuff into a smaller bag and checked in the offending piece. The baby must have sensed my angst, for she promptly started crying.

That was only check-in. Still to come for this lone adult travelling with two kids were the joys of security (removal of shoes, computer from case and baby from buggy, and sipping of sterilized water for the baby bottles, all accompanied by my normally well-behaved boy who decided it was time to whine), the purchase of the allowed liquids, and getting on to the plane. Oh, and then the small matter of the nine hours' flying time.

I was sleep-deprived and hassled, and yet, for a brief window of 25 minutes on the flight, I entered a holy space of peace and sanctuary. Jonathan was occupied with cartoons and Abigail was sleeping. As I calmed myself, I sought the gentle word of the Lord that he always wants to speak to his children.

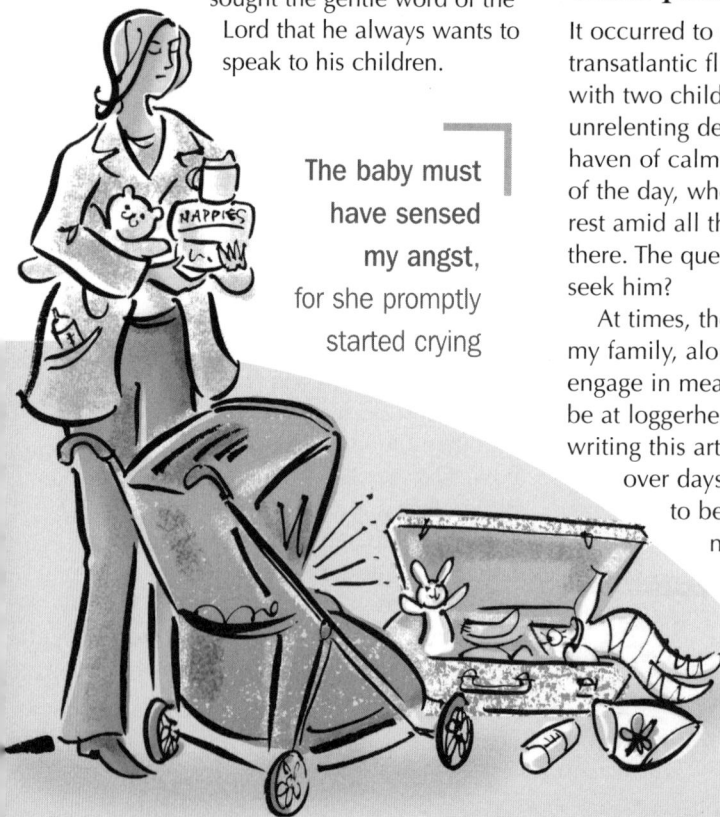

The baby must have sensed my angst, for she promptly started crying

He spoke to my heart of his love and care. He reassured me that even when I do not feel him nearby, he is there; that when I am caring for others and they are tired, cranky and demanding, he is not demanding. He may demand all of me—my thoughts, hopes, dreams, actions—but at that moment he was not placing any more weight on my shoulders. I could simply rest and be secure in his love.

Jonathan soon tired of the video and so it was back to constant conversation, but my oasis was enough. God's loving reassurance would nourish me for the rest of the journey.

Grace poured out

It occurred to me recently that my transatlantic flight is a snapshot of life with two children—seemingly unrelenting demands and yet a small haven of calm and hope. In the noon of the day, when I'm seeking a bit of rest amid all that is going on, God is there. The question is, can I, and do I, seek him?

At times, the competing needs of my family, alongside my desire to engage in meaningful work, seem to be at loggerheads. Even the exercise of writing this article has been stretched over days, with a baby needing to be fed and a young boy needing reassurance and loving discipline. My children's needs won't be lessening, just changing. My four-month-old needs milk, clean nappies, smiles, cuddles and interaction. My four-year-old needs the basics such as food, shelter and clothing, but also loads of loving attention and conversation, and especially answers for the never-changing question, 'Why?' No doubt, as the children get older, their needs will continue to change but not diminish—and of course I wouldn't want it any other way.

As a parent, my challenge is not merely to accommodate their needs but to embrace them—to become a living sacrifice, grace poured out. Admittedly, the grace sometimes feels like it is more squeezed than poured out, but so it is with the best wine or olive oil.

Two passages from Paul's first letter to the Corinthians are bringing me wisdom and hope during these years of early parenthood. The first is a command and the other a promise. The command comes in the midst of Paul's instructions to the Corinthians over various matters, such as the married or single life, the rights and freedoms of believers, the ways and practices of worship. While discussing whether or not to eat food that has been sacrificed to idols, Paul says, 'So whether you eat or drink or whatever you do, do it all for the glory of God' (10:31, TNIV).

In the noon of the day, this is my challenge—to do all for the glory of God, living in response to this command, sheltering under its canopy and covering. Thereby I may have a life attitude of servanthood and grace, seeking to love others more than myself, whether they are my husband, children, au pair or those I come in contact with in the community.

Do I always achieve this aim? As my husband can tell you in full detail, I fail regularly. Indeed, it just takes writing an article on spirituality to see how much of the 'old self' still needs putting off (see, for example, 2 Corinthians 5:17; Romans 6.6). But Christ living in me is forming a new

---

... even when I do not feel him nearby, he is there

---

creation. Tiny pieces are being added through the little things of life—for example, when I jump up from my computer without muttering as my son employs delaying tactics in his nightly quest to stay awake, or when I listen to a friend in need, even though I find her draining and I'm already low on sleep.

The light of eternity

As my husband is a historian and royalist, we recently went to Osborne House on the Isle of Wight. Our visit made a deep impression on my son, and not because of the army bunkers that Prince Albert constructed for his children or the vast collections of insects—rather, because there Queen Victoria died.

Jonathan seems fascinated by death. Perhaps he encounters more dying because he is the son of a vicar; perhaps it's just one of the phases children go through in discovering how the world works. I want to give him answers to his questions of 'Why?' but I do struggle to find an adequate response when we are three or four 'whys' into a sequence. 'Why do we

... there will come a time of **no more death or tears or pain or suffering**

die?' We just do. Everything that is living will die one day. Yes, it's sad. 'Why did Queen Victoria die?' She was old and it was her time to die. Yes, she died on 22 January, one day after Mommy's birthday, but many, many years ago. Yes, it was sad. Yes, we all die. And it's not how God wanted it to be. 'Why?' Well, that goes back to a long, long time ago, when people called Adam and Eve were living. They didn't do what God wanted, and so death came into the world. But you know Jesus? He died,

too, but his was a good death. Because when he died, he made it so that we can live for ever.

Usually then the 'whys' will cease for a time.

I don't mind that Jonathan is learning about death. It is part of this life, even though we are prone to hide it away until it roars into our lives, unbidden. As Christians, though, we know the end of the story, that there will come a time of no more death or tears or pain or suffering.

It's this eternal perspective that the second passage in 1 Corinthians provides: 'For now we see only a reflection in a mirror; then we shall see face to face. Now I know in part; then I shall know fully, even as I am fully known' (13:12). Just imagine—if in heaven my son were to ask me 'Why?' I could give him the complete answer!

I love the thought of an embodied exchange, of our seeing 'face to face', and of knowing fully, just as God already knows all that we are. For although our life on earth may be filled with fragments, one day it will be gloriously complete. Isn't it amazing that the One who is omniscient will share this knowledge with us?

Living with this eternal perspective can give us the hope, strength, grace and determination to be Christ to all those around us, whether they are the airline check-in staff or the questioning little boy. May we be empowered to spread his sweet scent, whatever stage of life we find ourselves in. ■

Life's noontide hour

Margaret Silf is an ecumenical lay Christian committed to working across and beyond the traditional denominational divides. Formerly employed in the computer industry, she now devotes her time to writing and facilitating retreats and workshops on aspects of Christian spirituality.

Two images come vividly to mind when I think of 'noontide'. The first is a memory of climbing the hills of Cumbria, resting at the summit to gaze at the landscape spread out below and enjoy a hard-earned packed lunch. The second is an image of noontide in the deserts of central Australia, in the burning midday heat and the full force of the sunlight. Both images continue to draw me into deeper reflection on the seasons of my own life—especially the noontide season.

... **reflection on the seasons of my own life**

Hills have always fascinated me. There is something about the desire to reach the top of a hill. What is it that drives us to keep striving towards the peak? Obviously there is a curiosity to see the view from the summit, even though we may have already seen it a thousand times in books and on postcards. We want to see it for ourselves and let it become part of who we are.

Then there is the satisfaction of achievement. We have to climb the peak, as the mountaineers always say, 'because it is there'. We want to push ourselves to the limits, just to see whether or not we can. There is a desire to be 'on top'. At its best, this is human nature trying to reach a personal best. At its worst, it can indicate a dangerous drivenness. Both are present, or at least latent, in the noontide of our lives—a healthy curiosity about all that still lies undiscovered in the future and a determination to achieve all we can as the years of our lives slip by.

The top of a hill is the landmark that divides the climb up from the way down. It marks a very definite change of direction. It is the resting point between the first and second halves of our day and of our lives. What do we find at the summit? What does it reveal about where we have come from and where we might be going?

Perhaps I can invite you to sit down awhile with me as we unpack the sandwiches, take out the thermos flask and enjoy the hour 'at the top'. When I reached this particular season in my own life, I was in full-time employment in the computer industry. I had 'climbed' my own rockfaces and been through my own struggles to gain and hold on to a competitive job, and I had the great good fortune to have a home-based contract, which meant that I could arrange my working hours around the care of my daughter.

> ... curiosity about all that still lies **undiscovered in the future**

There seemed to be no choice except staying on the treadmill of daily work

But as any working mum will know, this brought with it the perpetual tension between the demands of work and the requirements of parenting. Like many mothers in the same position, I often felt I was failing on both counts. As a Christian, I often wondered whether this was really 'God's will', but there seemed to be no choice except staying on the treadmill of daily work as I knew it.

When we get to Australia, I will share with you something of how the light changed, but for now, let's just take a look at the view we have climbed so far to see. When I look down from my noonday peak, I see all the fields spread out below me. Some are doing fine, with good crops and ripe fruits. Some are dry and sterile. Some of my life's projects have taken wings. Some have been miserable failures that I don't even want to think about. Yet from up here I can, and must, see them all, just as they are.

Then a strange thing happens: it gradually dawns on me that they all belong to the big picture. What I thought were failures were actually learning opportunities, providing the compost for the new growth in other parts of my life. Without them I would not be who I am. In fact, the failures were probably more important to my growth in God than any of my 'successes', real or imagined. Our failures can be God's fast-track routes into our inner depths, precisely at the points where we need God most.

Another thing that the summit view reveals is the large number of winding pathways that lead up the hill. I have taken only one of them and I have agonized about which way to take at every fork in the path. Now, from up here, I can see that whichever path I might have chosen anywhere along the way, God would have been there with me, guiding and nourishing me, prompting, correcting and encouraging. 'I am the Way,' I hear God whisper. 'You don't have to take the path alone, but I will make your path my own, and together we will find the way home to my heart and yours.'

... the failures were probably more important to my growth in God than any of my 'successes', real or imagined

Experience is heightened and from here, we feel, we can reach for the stars—but **what goes up must come down**

Great dreams can be dreamed, here on the mountaintop. Experience is heightened and from here, we feel, we can reach for the stars—but what goes up must come down. The vision may happen on the hilltop but the outworking of that vision, its *real*-ization, can only happen down in the valley, where real life is really lived by real people in a real world. And so, after we have been refreshed in our peak moments, God turns our sights to the way back down. There is work to be done in the valley. Noontide was just a flavour of all that is still to come.

A dramatic change of scene now, as we fly south to Uluru in the heart of the Australian central desert. This landscape, too, gave me the gift of a noontide revelation. It was my first day there and I tentatively set forth to walk a little way through the red sand and the low shrubs of the outback. The image that captured my imagination that day was the power of light and shadow. Every growing thing was anchored to its own black shadow, so clearly defined and so very beautiful. I couldn't put my camera down, so enthralled was I by the strength and definition of these powerful shadows and so captivated by the sheer glory of the light. Perhaps it was in that place and at that time of my life that I truly began to understand how God's call and God's dream can penetrate our depths in ways we never expected, setting our own efforts into a new perspective and transforming our dreams into an authentic call to turn them into action. The light illuminates us in new ways but it also reveals the full force of our shadow side.

Every growing thing was anchored to its own black shadow, so clearly defined and so very beautiful

Now, in hindsight, I know that it was certainly the right choice at the right time

With a clarity I had never dared to hope for, I knew that the time for change had arrived in my life. I could see, unmasked, the fears that held me in a routine job that had actually passed its sell-by date. The noontide sun revealed the persistent call of the requests from people to write more and to offer days of reflection or retreats. I had reached a decision point. If I wanted to honour these requests and my own heart's promptings, I had to take the risk of letting go of a secure job and pay cheque, and set out along a road both unknown and unpredictable. But in the light of that noonday sun, not just in Uluru but in my times of quiet prayer, I knew in my heart that there was no contest. God doesn't easily take 'No' for an answer.

Now, in hindsight, I know that it was certainly the right choice at the right time. I found a quite unexpected way down the mountain, and I am overwhelmed with wonder when I think of the thrilling and challenging landscapes that this 'descent' into the second half of life has disclosed. I thank God for every moment, even though the way has not been without its tumbles and fears and questions.

The miracle is this: the noonday light doesn't fade but it takes up residence in our hearts if we let it. Then the summit view turns out not to be a fleeting vision but a glimpse of what is more real than anything we can grasp with our 'morning' minds. Don't be afraid to embrace the changes of noon. They come from God and they lead to God. ■

Embracing God's World

'Embracing God's World' (BRF, 2007) is the revised edition of Joyce Huggett's personal selection of prayers, first published in 1996. It includes many of her own prayers as well as contributions by other writers. Here are some of Joyce's prayers from the first section of the book, 'Enjoying intimacy with God'.

Hungry and thirsty for God's presence

Dear Lord,
teach me to pray.
For just as the deer pants for cool water
so my heart hungers for you.
My soul is parched and dry;
I thirst for your presence, my living Lord.
I will carve out a place for you.
Lord, hear my prayer
in that place,
in every place—
come to me and meet me.

Your servant is listening

Speak, Lord, for your servant is listening.
O, Lord, my heart is ready,
my mind awake, attentive, alert;
my spirit open and ardent,
abandoning all else,
holding itself in leash,
straining the eye of faith,
hearkening for your step, distant and nearer,
leaping with love,
throbbing loudly, yet lying still.
Speak, Lord, for your servant is listening.

At peace

You are my peace, O Lord.
From the thousand wearinesses of the day-to-day,
from the disappointments,
from the nervous and senseless haste,
I turn to you
and am at peace.
The clamour dies.
I spring to life in the sunshine of your presence.
Even so, come, Lord Jesus,
to this heart of mine.

God's love

Father,
I pray that out of the wealth of your glory
you will strengthen my inner being with your Spirit,
so that Christ will make his home in my heart,
and so that I may have my roots in love
and make love the foundation
of my entire existence.
I pray that you will reveal to me
just how broad and long,
how high and deep
the love of Christ is,
so that I may be filled to overflowing
with the very nature of Christ.

Lord, your love is a persevering love
that brings me back,
that renews a sense of perspective,
that woos and wins me again and again.
For this undeserved, unearned gift
I feel eternally grateful.

Music for the soul:

Calvary noon

Gordon Giles is vicar of St Mary Magdalene's Church, Enfield, north London. He contributes to BRF's 'New Daylight' notes and has also written 'The Music of Praise' (2002), 'The Harmony of Heaven' (2003) and 'O Come, Emmanuel' (2005) for BRF.

Crucifixus etiam pro nobis; sub Pontio Pilato passus et sepultus est.

He was crucified also for us under Pontius Pilate; he suffered and was buried.

TEXT: FROM THE NICENE CREED
MUSIC: ANTONIO LOTTI (1666–1740)

Noon is a very important time of day in the Bible and has great significance. It is a time of prayer or conversion, and of darkness. Elijah's contest with the priests of Baal takes place around noon (1 Kings 18:26–27), and so we may think of it as a time when God has the victory over opposition and idolatry. For the prophets Jeremiah and Zephaniah, noon is the time of attack in battle, when judgment shall be meted out (Jeremiah 6:4; 20:16; Zephaniah 2:4). Yet, for Amos, noon is the time when darkness shall fall, indicating a reversal of the norm, a turning upside down of things as they are (Amos 8:9). In the New Testament, Jesus meets the Samaritan woman at the well around noon (John 4:6) and, for Peter, it is a customary time to pray: on one day, while doing so, he has a vision in which he is told that all living creatures are clean (Acts 10:9). For Paul, noon heralds a blinding light on the road to Damascus, a light to change his life and the world after him (22:6).

The most important noon, however, must be the high noon of Good Friday, when 'darkness came over the whole land [for three hours] until three in the afternoon' (Matthew 27:45). The darkness of noon is a fulfilment of prophecy and an indication that the world is upturned: things will never be the same again, judgment is here, and also salvation. As Christ hangs on the cross, crucified publicly in shame, degradation and injustice, the sun is eclipsed as if to hide his humiliation from the sight of God himself. A solar eclipse is a strange phenomenon: the sky turns dark, the wind seems to drop, the birds refuse to sing as 'night' descends so uncannily. It must have been like that on Good Friday lunchtime when our Lord was nailed up to die: 'I danced on a Friday when the sky turned black, it's hard to dance with the devil on your back,' as Sydney Carter put it in the modern hymn 'Lord of the Dance'.

A noonday eclipse turns one day into two, just as noon itself cuts the day in half, dividing morning from afternoon. The very word 'afternoon' is pertinent and, when we think of the crucifixion as having taken place at noon, we are reminded that we live in the afternoon of salvation: the time after redemption has been won on the cross. For there is a sense in which the cross is neither the beginning nor the end of our salvation, but our midpoint. As some say, we live in the 'now but not yet' of salvation: the victory has been won, but we still await the final closing of the eternal day, when Christ shall return in triumph to complete the work he began on the cross on Good Friday noon.

For many, the noontide timing of the crucifixion is simply a statement of temporal fact. No one can dispute the historical truth of the crucifixion—it is attested in texts that are, frankly, anti-Christian—but the noontide timing also has spiritual significance as the turning point of the day, the turning point of history's day, or even the pivot of his story. So there is more to the crucifixion than the bald fact that Christ died at noon.

We find a similar dimension when we consider sacred music. Antonio Lotti took a brief statement from the Creed about the death of Christ and made it say far more than simply 'Christ was crucified also for us under Pontius Pilate; he suffered and was buried'. If you listen to Lotti's setting

---

The darkness of noon

is a fulfilment of prophecy and an indication that the world is upturned...

---

of these words (his most famous work), there is no doubt of the significance of the death of Christ. The Creed tells us what to believe but Lotti's music tells us what to feel.

Although born in Germany, Lotti was Venetian, and became *primo maestro di capella* (director of chapel music) at St Mark's, Venice, in 1736. He wrote music for banquets given by the Doge, operas and sacred music. He composed many settings of the

Crucifixus, of which his eight-voice version is the best-known. It is taken from a five-movement setting of the Creed, in F major, written during a leave of absence in Dresden, 1717–19. Most of the work is in four parts but

It is not simply that Christ was crucified...

the choir divides into eight for this brief but moving section of the Creed.

It is not easy to sing: each choral entry is exposed as the sound builds, adding height and width, the musical texture swelling as the statement of fact ('*crucifixus*') becomes a foundation of faith ('*etiam pro nobis*'). It is not simply that Christ was crucified; what is significant and heart-rending is that he was crucified *for us*. Such is music's ability to speak and heal and convert at levels below and above mere words. By the time we reach '*et sepultus est*' ('and was buried'), two-thirds of the way into this two-minute work, we are drawn in emotionally so that we are truly mourning the death of Christ— and mourn it we should, sinners that we are, for his death is for us.

Yet, just as noon and afternoon depend on each other, there can be no crucifixion without resurrection or

resurrection without death. Lotti's *Crucifixus*, sung out of context as it so often is, implies that there is death without resurrection. The text that follows it should never be overlooked: '*et resurrectio tertia diae*' ('and rose again on the third day'). So, when we hear this beautiful music, let us never forget that the crucifixion and burial it describes are not the end of the story, but the beginning of the new life opened up for us in Jesus Christ, our risen Lord. ■

PRAYER

Father God, there is no greater love than that you show us in the sending of your Son Jesus Christ to die for our sins at the high noon of world history. Bless and heal us as we contemplate your mercy, and enable us to walk always in the eternal light of Christ's resurrection hope. Amen

Readings for reflection
Matthew 27:32–54

Music to listen to
Crucifixus by Lotti. It is widely available on recordings such as *Passiontide at St Paul's* (ref: Hyperion CDA66916); directed by John Scott; organist Andrew Lucas, 1997.

How icons can speak to us

Sister Esther is a member of the Vita et Pax Benedictine Community at Turvey Abbey, Bedfordshire, and a founder of the British Association of Iconographers. Among her community activities, she runs icon-painting workshops and paints icons for individual commissions and churches. She is affiliated to the Greek Catholic Melkite Church and is involved in promoting an understanding of Orthodoxy, from which the tradition of icons emerged.

Icons are much in fashion in the Western world of art and prayer. Some people who encounter them are often taken by some quality in them, while they seem nonsensical to others. Many who encounter them abroad in a country whose main Christian practice is that of the Orthodox Church come back enhanced by encountering them. Once they have begun to understand their meaning, they often wish they had known more before their trip. If we wish to use icons in our personal prayer life, it is good to know something of their meaning and how we can use them.

> Icons are painted to lead us into the **inner room of prayer**

The meaning of icons

The word 'iconography' comes from the Greek words for 'image' and 'writing'. The practice of 'image writing' is quite different from Western art. Since the Renaissance, Western art has been influenced by (among other ideas and ideals) naturalism and an interest in how things work—for example, artists have studied anatomy. This is not so with icons. Originating within the liturgical and philosophical setting of Byzantine culture and life, icons aim to express the spiritual and idealistic vision of Orthodoxy. Their aim includes conscious awareness of the spiritualization or 'deification' (in Orthodox terminology) of matter; the pledge of an already redeemed creation and the coming victory over a fallen one; the expression of the future unity of the whole of creation; and a manifestation of humankind's spiritual power to redeem creation through beauty and art.

> ... **simplicity of form**, calmness of movement, rhythm of line and joyfulness of colour

An icon is much more than merely a visual teaching aid or picture

The sensory aspect of corruptible flesh thus becomes spiritualized, and in their icons saints are seen as being reformed to their true and original being, as intended by God in Christ. The artist seeks to express the divine nature with which Christ is endowed and the inner spiritual beauty with which the saints are animated. When looking at the image of Christ, the mother of God or a saint, therefore, one is looking not at an earthly portrait but at a person transfigured in Christ—an image of the invisible.

An icon is much more than merely a visual teaching aid or picture; it has about it a sacramental quality. Within Orthodoxy, icons are venerated (but not worshipped) just as the Bible is held in honour and revered. The Council of Constantinople in AD860 stated, 'That which the book tells us in words, the icon announces to us by colour and makes present to us' and St John Damascene affirmed that 'icons are theology not only in words but in images'. How this is done is expressed in understanding the art of icons.

The art of icons

The human exterior—its clothing, hair and the parts of the body—are not represented literally but expressed stylistically, using haloes, lines and specific postures. For example, clothing, though expressed logically, takes on geometrical forms with a pattern of lights and lines on its folds. Faces frequently have thin mouths and large eyes, which lack brilliance. The hair, the wrinkles and the whole of the body of the saint show a sense of unification and convey harmony and serenity.

This feeling also applies to the subject matter—the supreme and best-known example being Andrei Rublev's *Trinity* (painted 1408–25), referred to by the Council of a

Hundred Chapters (a 16th-century Russian church council) as the 'icon of icons'. This icon conveys a simplicity of form, calmness of movement, rhythm of line and joyfulness of colour springing from an inner harmony—a combination aimed at by all icons.

Furthermore, there is in icons little attempt to depict landscape or architecture in correct proportion. Instead, the landscape may show a transformed cosmos with rocks thrusting outwards and upwards, and buildings may be painted with inverse perspective to draw the onlooker into what the image affirms and expresses.

Icons and our own prayer life

Icons are an aid not only in liturgical settings but also privately in nourishing the individual's inner world of prayer and contemplation. St John Damascene, a great defender of icons during the iconoclastic controversy of 717–754, said, 'When my thoughts torment me and prevent me from reading, I go to Church. My gaze is held and my soul is moved to praise God. I contemplate the martyr's valour... and his zeal inflames me... I adore and pray to God through the martyr's intercession and communion.'

It is also recorded that Rublev and his co-workers would sometimes spend hours just contemplating what they had painted. Henri Nouwen, in his book *Behold the Beauty of the Lord: Praying with Icons* (Ave Maria Press, 1987), has written, 'Icons are painted to lead us into the inner room of prayer and bring us close to the heart of God. Every time I entrust myself to these images, move beyond my curious questions about their origin, history and artistic value and let them speak to me in their own language, they draw me into closer communion with the God of love.'

Here is a way of reflecting on the Holy Trinity icon (with thanks to Sister Johanna for her helpful encouragement).

... a person transfigured in Christ—an image of the invisible

Looking at the icon

The source of Andrei Rublev's icon is Genesis 18, which relates how Abraham gave hospitality to three men who appeared by the oak of Mamre. The three men are depicted in the icon as winged angels and the oak of Mamre as the tree of life. Abraham's dwelling represents the Church. Rublev has abandoned many traditional details in this icon, such as Abraham and Sarah serving the angels with food and numerous dishes on the table. Instead we see only the three angels sitting around the table in profound silence with their heads silently inclined towards one another. The table becomes an altar with only the eucharistic cup in the centre.

The angel on the left, blessing the

© Visual Arts Library (London)/Alamy

Letting it speak to you

Rublev was ordered to paint this icon in 1425 by Abbot Nikon so that 'by contemplation of the Holy Trinity, the eyes of the monks might be turned away from hateful dissensions of this world'. Let something of the stillness of this icon speak to you. Gaze on the angels, silently listening to one another. Listen to what the icon is saying:

Come now, little person, turn aside for a while from the tumult of your thoughts. Put aside the weight of your cares and rest a while in God.
ST ANSELM

cup, is thought to represent God the Father, while the centre angel is clothed in the traditional colours depicting Christ and wearing a priestly stole. The angel on the right, then, represents the Holy Spirit, clothed in the life-giving colour of green. The tranquil colours, overlaid with paler tones and white highlights, the circular movement in the icon and the geometrical structures create a movement of unity and life, which speaks of the life of the Trinity.

Continue to let your gaze rest on the icon until you see not just with your eyes and intellect but also with your soul and heart. Let yourself be absorbed in this sacred encounter.

O holy life-giving Trinity, present in all places, treasury of blessing, come and dwell within me and calm, refresh and renew me.
ADAPTATION OF ORTHODOX PRAYER

Reflecting on this icon can be an experience of serenity, of timelessness, of the eternal now— one avenue to that experience for which we all inwardly yearn. ■

Angels
unawares

Patricia Rantisi has spent most of her life abroad, first as a missionary in Peru, then in the Middle East for nearly 40 years. She has written many articles and two books about the Palestinian/Israeli conflict ('Blessed are the Peacemakers', Eagle, 2003 and 'Miriam's Legacy', Author House, 2007)

The Lord appeared to Abraham near the great trees of Mamre while he was sitting at the entrance to his tent in the heat of the day. Abraham looked up and saw three men standing nearby. When he saw them, he hurried from the entrance of his tent to meet them and bowed low to the ground.

GENESIS 18:1–2 (NIV)

Here was Abraham having a midday rest, probably enjoying 40 winks. After all, he was a very old man, a hundred years old. I wonder how he knew that these were angelic men, as they were probably dressed in the normal Bedouin robes of the time. In any case, the generous hospitality he offered them would have been the same as for any other visitors—a bowl of water to wash their feet, something to eat and drink and a place to rest. Moreover, it was not a bit of bread and cheese but a lavish feast that Abraham made for them, treating them as if he was their humble servant and it was a great honour for him to serve them.

Do we have here a prophetic picture of the Trinity? Maybe. Certainly we have a picture of Middle Eastern hospitality which is the same today as it was those thousands of years ago. The writer to the book of Hebrews in the New Testament was probably thinking of this story when he wrote, 'Do not forget to entertain strangers, for by so doing some people have entertained angels without knowing it' (Hebrews 13:2).

Having lived in the Middle East myself for 38 years, I have had first-hand experience of this hospitality, both as guest and as hostess. My husband and I ran a home for

Middle Eastern people have so much to teach us

Hospitality is given to strangers without questions for three days

underprivileged Palestinian children for 30 years in the city of Ramallah, ten miles from Jerusalem. We employed a cook, so there was always plenty to go round and any visitors who turned up unannounced were given a hearty meal. But it was a work of faith, so by the end of the month we never knew exactly where the money would come from to pay the bills. We proved the Lord's promises time and time again for the

supply of all our needs.

My husband, Audeh, was Palestinian, so I learnt from him in the early days the basic rudiments of the Arabic language and customs. He instilled in me, with much patience, how to treat strangers. Always welcome them in with the words 'Ahlan Wa Sahlan', which literally means 'You have come to your own place and the way is made ready before you.' Next, *never* ask them if they want a drink, as they will always politely refuse; just give them a soft drink at first, coffee later. Then, if it is near a meal time, invite them to partake of the meal with you. They will refuse again but you have to insist. All this for uninvited visitors—imagine how we treated invited guests!

We were always entertaining strangers. In fact, my husband was horrified at the English custom of preparing exact portions of food for the number of people invited, and talking to people on the doorstep rather than inviting them in.

I remember one day, in Ramallah, a young man arrived wearing rather dishevelled clothes and sandals that were literally threadbare. He was English and said he had been doing volunteer work in Nazareth (which is a long way from Ramallah). We offered him some newer sandals, which he refused, and gave him food and lodging. He did not have much to say so we did not question him. The next morning, I gave him breakfast and he went on his way. Later, I took

down the breadbasket that I kept on the top of the fridge, to find a large wad of paper money, which was just what we needed at the time. Was the stranger an angel? He had not left his name or address.

(Here, I might add a note of an unspoken Middle Eastern custom: hospitality is given to strangers without questions for three days. After that, questions may be asked! Actually, I have never had to put this into practice.)

My most significant memory is of one evening after we had retired to bed early and I was reading about Abraham in Genesis 18. I remarked to my husband that the Palestinians had still retained the custom of generous hospitality, just as in the days of Abraham, but that in Israel (except for

... not a bit of bread and cheese but a lavish feast

the so-called Sabra Jews, who originate from the Middle East) they had lost this custom and were very suspicious of strangers. This is because the majority of Israelis are immigrants from Europe and America, and Westerners seem to lack this basic instinct of hospitality.

After our discussion, there was a sudden knock on our back door. You may imagine my amazement when I opened it to find three strangers. They said they were lost and their car had broken down. I remember preparing a meal for them at midnight while their car was being fixed and then my husband showed them the way to Jerusalem.

Up to a few years ago, our home was open for visitors of any faith— Muslims, Jews and Christians, who are all 'children of Abraham'. Nowadays it is more difficult because of the political divisions. Yet Middle Eastern people have so much to teach us, as Westerners, about the way that we treat strangers. Who knows, we may be entertaining angels unawares! ■

Pray not for Arab or Jew,
for Palestinian or Israeli,
but pray rather for ourselves,
that we may not divide them in our prayers
but keep them both together in our hearts.

And that will be heaven

and that will be heaven

and that will be heaven
at last   the first unclouded
seeing

*   to stand like the sunflower*
turned full face to the sun   drenched
with light   in the still centre
held   while the circling planets
hum with an utter joy

*   seeing and knowing*
at last   in every particle
seen and known   and not turning
away

*   never turning away*
again
EVANGELINE PATERSON

Spiritual direction:

Learning to walk in step with God

Jenny Hellyer is a spiritual director, musician, mother of two teenagers and the wife of a vicar in Oxford.

As a twin, I learned from my earliest years how to be alongside another. Passed down the family history are stories of the hours my brother and I spent communicating non-verbally as we sat in a huge twin pram.

Later, as a musician, I developed a love of accompanying, particularly for stringed instrument players. As their pianist, I both set the stage for their gifts and added a dimension of my own. Part of my work today is still to encourage young people in their music performance skills, lifting note-learning into music-

Where is God in your situation?

making. This is something of an analogy for the ministry of spiritual direction, where, under God, the listener is sensitive both to the words of the one sharing and also to the inner prompting of the Spirit. Together, we discern the work of God in the other's life, and life becomes more in tune with the Lord.

In my teenage years, I was drawn to the life of Job: I

The work of spiritual direction is more formalized and intentional

articulate their sorrows and joys. Knowing personally the experience of Jesus' healing gave me a quiet confidence in his intention and power to restore lives.

I lived in the Lee Abbey community for several years. This was a formative time where, in a climate of hard work, encouragement and prayer, I often found myself in the privileged position of listening and praying for others. One or two asked if I would consider being their spiritual director, but I had not much idea what that meant.

Some years later, when my two children were still quite small, I prayed about what God might have in mind for me, and I sensed that his call to me was not to do more counselling training but to move into spiritual direction. I embarked on a short course in Nottingham, and later a diocesan course in Oxford. The passion in my heart was for the connection we all need with God in our daily living.

A key question in this ministry is 'Where is God in your situation?' and a key encouragement is 'God is with you'. One of the loveliest biblical accounts of this process is the walk of those

could identify with his suffering. My family life had crumbled and then my mother died in a car accident. I had just turned eleven. Where was God? Where was anyone who could sit with such losses? It was years before I could begin to process and find the presence of God in this story. As he led me into healing, I found that I was often sitting with others who needed to be able to disciples on the Emmaus road (Luke 24:13–35). As they are trying to make sense of their recent traumatic experience, Jesus draws alongside, listens and, finally, makes himself known. He restores faith and a sense of being loved, and he gives them all they need to be his resurrection ambassadors. They become aware of God with them.

As a vicar's wife, I have spontaneous opportunities to encourage my friends at St Matthew's, and they do the same for me, but the work of spiritual direction is more formalized and intentional. In deciding to come for an hour next week, Sue is wanting to commit herself to her walk with God and to welcome a companion into this mysterious and wonderful journey. It's not problem solving, although life brings its issues; it's more a time to reflect on external and internal events and to see their significance in the light of what God is doing. I never cease to be in awe of the blessing that the Lord bestows on these holy encounters.

The New Testament is full of exhortations to love one another, and direction is an expression of his purpose that we hold one another in this love. We usually begin in quietness or with a biblical reflection and prayer as we remember God's desire to accompany us. My role of listening, both to Sue and to God, enables a certain exploration for Sue. As she talks or pauses for thought, something may clarify; often an inkling becomes more definite.

At times this leads to a new decision. In the safety of our place and time together, God may uncover something that has wounded her, or an issue that needs to be touched by his love. I am sometimes on the edge of my seat—it's not for the faint-hearted! To be accepted and heard are such precious things, which we all can offer to each other, and in the context of direction they are the doorways for God to come with his Spirit's wisdom, love and challenge. The rhythm of meeting together every six to eight weeks means that there is a sense of being held in the journey. Sue can leave my house, pondering the hour we had together, and dare to stay open to what God may be saying or doing in her life.

Spiritual directors are as varied as people in any other work role. I would share some of my own story of life with people if it might encourage

> As she talks or pauses for thought, something may clarify; **often an inkling becomes more definite**

them. I see that encouragement as a huge part of this ministry. But the term 'direction' is misleading if we think we will be told how to do things! No, the prayerful encounter where Sue brings her life before another and God means that she can become more honest, finding courage to own her walk and to go with God. This is particularly precious for those in leadership positions, where isolation can lead to loneliness, lack of clarity and even stored-up issues, because there is no one to go to. None of us needs to be in such a place.

In her book *Holy Listening*, Margaret Guenther offers three pictures of spiritual direction. The first is that of *hospitality*. This is a hallmark of the

The director watches, waits, encourages and blesses

We are all learners, and being directed keeps us humble

church and a reflection of God himself, who welcomes us into the greatest relationship we could imagine. I welcome people not just to my physical home. Part of my being able to give full attention to others is to have paid attention to my own 'home', my own walk with God, so as to have something to offer in terms of spiritual hospitality. I am also resourced by a supervision group of other directors, where we seek to offer wisdom and grace to each other's ministries. I find that if I am wrongly preoccupied (and yes, that happens), I am unable to be fully present to the one who comes. Jesus had an astonishing ability to receive people just where they were (even up a tree, in the case of Zacchaeus); he also withdrew to be alone in God's presence.

The second image is that of the *teacher*. I taught for a few years before doing a theology degree and I learned that a good teacher needs to respond to the present needs of pupils even while holding out future possibilities. I recall abandoning a music lesson in order to explain how paragraphs work, for a panicked GCSE class. Jesus poured out life-giving teaching using not just facts but stories, pictures and humour. Often the Holy Spirit gives insight to a director which is based on their own knowledge but goes beyond that knowledge. We are all learners, and being directed keeps us humble.

The third image is of the *midwife*. This is a useful image because a midwife will tell you that she is not creating new life, but simply (or not so simply) facilitating it. What a privilege this is! God is the creator of life; the director watches, waits, encourages and blesses the life that God brings. It is a holy business.

In our fast-living culture, there has grown a desire to find connectedness once again. To give ourselves permission to share at depth will, in itself, be like having a drink in the heat of the day. Why are we reluctant to seek out the oasis God loves us to experience? The pressures around us mean that sitting with God or with each other, listening attentively, feels countercultural. My favourite word at the moment is 'intentional'; I sense that in the current climate Christians need to be brave and purposefully embrace a more reflective way of living. As Jesus experienced enormous pressures, both of opposition and of spiritual battle, did he just go faster? No! He intentionally lived out of the oasis of his Father's love, and out of the depth of relationship with the few disciples he loved and was called to lead.

What might you learn from a director? Some of us find it hard to ask anyone to 'be there' for us, so the first thing we learn is to become less self-reliant. We also find that we are loved as we are heard. You may think, 'She has no idea what a mess my spiritual life is!' But this is the second thing: we come with the poverty of our lives, only to find that our loving God graciously embraces it and loves to use it for his glory. How amazing is that? Then, gradually, we come to direction as much for him as for ourselves: we actually do want to know him more and for his kingdom to grow in and through us.

In my experience, both of being directed (by a wise and kind member of an Anglican Community) and of directing others, spiritual direction is an opportunity, a space for God. What could be more exciting than to see life as an adventure with him? ■

Embrace a more reflective way of living

··

Further reading

Holy Listening by Margaret Guenther (DLT, 1992)
Spiritual Direction by Peter Ball (SPCK, 2003)

St Benedict:

Rules for a good life

Henry Wansbrough has been a regular contributor to 'New Daylight' and 'Guidelines'. He is a Benedictine monk of Ampleforth and member of the Pontifical Biblical Commission. For a dozen years he was Master of St Benet's Hall in Oxford, and served as Chairman of the Oxford Theology Faculty.

'What is a monk?' asked the four-year-old. 'Someone who enjoys praying,' replied his mother as she introduced me. There have been monks since the earliest years of Christianity, men (and women) who gave up everything to live a carefree life in the desert where they could simply be with the Lord. They wanted to step out of the 'rat-race' and live with Jesus, the gospel values their only guide and preoccupation. This way of life took different forms for different people, some solitary, some living together in groups, some fairly dotty—like those who isolated themselves in a sort of nest on top of a pillar, or those who prayed for hours immersed up to their necks in the cold waters of the North Sea.

Soon after the fall of the Roman Empire, a Roman lawyer (possibly a dropout from law school, but certainly someone with a capacity for coherent thinking) wrote a *Rule for Monks*. We know little about him, though legends of miracles and visions gathered round him. A century afterwards, the busy Pope Gregory the Great, who longed to escape the cares of office and become a monk, wrote a life of this man, calling him Benedict, which means 'the Blessed One'. The stories he tells about Benedict bear an uncanny resemblance to those told of Old Testament prophets, especially Elijah and Elisha, and of the Fathers (and Mothers) of the Desert. Everything we really know about him comes from the *Rule* he wrote, which is not the stuff of legend at all, but luminously down to earth.

The author of the *Rule* builds on earlier attempts to regulate monastic life, and comparison with earlier documents shows the wisdom of the subtle but significant changes he quietly introduced. Perhaps the most dominant trait is the pervading atmosphere of calm joy at 'running in the way of God's commands'. The uncommon good sense of the *Rule* caused it to spread rapidly, adopted by monks everywhere, until it was the basis of almost all monastic life in the West. In it we see a wise and experienced guide, nourished on the scriptures and above all on the Gospels, alive to all human foibles and weaknesses, leavened by a gentle humour which allows him to poke fun even at himself: 'We read that wine is altogether not a thing for monks, but nowadays it does not seem possible to persuade them of this, so let us at least drink only moderately.'

The abbot is the father of the community and must act like a father: his first care is the physically, psychologically and emotionally sick and the wounded. He must not break the bruised reed, but must give the strong a goal to strive for. The monks should not carp at each other but should gently encourage one another. There is special consideration for the hungry young (they can eat earlier in the day) and for the zealous seniors (they should be given assistance in their tasks). The writer has some pet hates, and chief of them is grumbling: 'nothing is more destructive of a family'. In every person Christ must be seen,

What is a monk?
Someone who enjoys praying

but especially in the sick, the old and guests: the abbot washes the feet of a guest on arrival, but must not hesitate to ask a disruptive guest to leave!

It should be prescribed reading for every family, every office and every company, wherever people live and work together. But what has the *Rule for Monks* to do with noon, with the heat of the day, the time when

The pause for prayer makes sense of the work

business and work is at its height? The *Rule* knows about that, too. The monastic way is no escape into an easy life, for 'then are they truly monks if they earn their living by the work of their hands'.

There is a care for quality of work, and especially for the precious tools, which are to be treated 'like the sacred vessels of the altar'. Commercialism, however, is far from the aim: products should be available at a lower cost than in the common market. Any brother who gets puffed up with pride in his achievements and congratulates himself on his contribution to the community should unhesitatingly be reallocated.

Everything in moderation, and there must be a balance of work, meditative reading and formal prayer. In the 11th century, the monks of Cluny went wrong by evolving such splendour of choral prayer that there was no room for work. In the 13th, the Cistercians went wrong by such successful sheep farming that they got too rich. So at three evenly spaced moments during the working day (and noon is one of them) the monk should drop everything and pray. If a brother is working too far out in the fields to join in the choral prayer, he should simply stop, down tools and pray where he is, united in prayer with the others who pray in the same Spirit of God. The pause for prayer makes sense of the work; without the prayer, the work has no purpose.

Nothing should get in the way of this prayer, which Benedict calls 'the work of God'. The regulations for the choral office are thoughtful and precise but never fussy. At their heart is simplicity. The monk soon knows the psalter by heart, the familiarity and routine adding tranquillity to these precious moments. The oratory (no mention is made of a 'church'—far too grand) should be a place of silence, so that any monk can simply slip in and pray on his own. Nothing should be stored there: in the oratory the monk should be cocooned with God alone. Silent prayer in community should be short, simple and pure.

The pause for prayer at noon gives shape to the day and, in its turn, is enriched by this shape. Nor need it be confined to monks! The writer whom we call Benedict is not afraid of the sweat and toil of noontide; he builds it into a context whose timeless values transcend its transitory strains and tensions. ∎

Into the crucible:

Launde Abbey

Tim Blewett is Warden of Launde Abbey. He was previously Canon Residentiary of St Asaph Cathedral with responsibility as Diocesan Officer for Ministry, Diocesan Director of Ordinands and Adviser for Continuing Ministerial Education. He has served as a Chaplain to the Forces, having been mobilized as a Territorial Army Chaplain for Bosnia (1997–98) and Iraq (2003–04).

The Tudor-Elizabethan retreat house known as Launde Abbey is surrounded on three sides by higher ground so that it seems to rest in a bowl made by its parkland. That is the way I saw it when I first arrived at Launde. But then, one day, soon after I had become Warden, I was told by someone on retreat that I should not describe the landscape in which Launde sits as a bowl but rather as a crucible. They were, of course, right: a crucible describes not only the landscape but also what happens here. After all, a bowl is where things are mixed up, while a crucible is a place in which transformation happens. People who come to Launde are transformed!

I arrived at Launde as Warden three

years ago and in that time Launde has become a love affair for me. I have been transformed myself as I have had the privilege of travelling spiritually with so many people who come here. They come from all sorts of different backgrounds: faith, no faith and everything in between. It is a place in which new conversations and insights take place, and which continues to change people even after they have left. It is truly a place where the divine touches the human and the human touches the divine, allowing God to be glimpsed not just in the natural beauty of Launde but in people's lives.

All are welcome to Launde, whoever they are and whatever they have done. People are not judged but are offered Christian hospitality and support to become what they have been given by Christ to be. It is thus a space that cannot be contained by or limited to any one group of people. Christ did not limit the kinds of people with whom he shared his table, so nor should we. Everyone is on a journey; everyone needs encouragement on the way, so that they might reach their full potential— to be the person only they can be, and do the things that only they can do, in Christ's love, mercy, forgiveness, compassion, healing and grace. Perhaps it is not surprising, therefore, that Rowan Williams, the Archbishop of Canterbury, has described Launde as 'an oasis of calm within the turmoil of modern daily life' and has gone on to say that 'it is

a place of intense prayer where countless people—myself included—have benefited from being able to spend time apart'.

This has been the case ever since Launde was dedicated as a retreat house 50 years ago in 1958. It had been given the previous year by Mr and Mrs Coleman. I have discovered

They come from all sorts of different backgrounds: faith, no faith and everything in between

recently that the Colemans bought the house with its Georgian stables and estate in 1956 to be a country holiday centre for their factory workers in Leicester. This plan was not a success, however, as the workers preferred to go to the Lincolnshire coast rather than into the countryside of the

It is truly a place where the divine touches the human and **the human touches the divine**

... a place of prayer, of education and of hospitality

Leicestershire–Rutland border. The Colemans therefore gave Launde to the Bishop of Leicester and a Trust was created, establishing a retreat house.

While Launde was initially given to benefit the diocese and people of Leicestershire, it soon became known by others from further afield—and now has a national and even international reputation as one of the more beautiful retreat houses in the country. It has consequently become a place where individuals and groups come from all over the UK and beyond to find stillness, tranquillity and peace, which is provided by an undergirding of prayer within the Abbey (the daily offices, including Compline, are kept, and a daily Eucharist or Communion service celebrated). The prayer at Launde is further supported by a group of people who have dedicated themselves to praying both for those who live and work in the Abbey and also for all those who come to the Abbey.

When I arrived at Launde, I was very keen, as the Trustees were, to reaffirm that Launde's vocation is to be a retreat house providing a space into which everyone is welcome, and not just another conference centre. Launde thus reaffirmed that it was a place of prayer, of education and of hospitality. Everything that is done here is done to enable those aims. People can come to Launde via our 'open' programme of retreats, which range from individually guided silent retreats to themed retreats, working with people such as John Bell and Margaret Silf. They also come as part of a group such as a cell or parish group. Launde is not limited to Christian groups, however, but is also used by other faith and secular groups. Still others will come to Launde as individuals who just want to 'do their own thing', resting and relaxing in the spacious gardens and house.

Ethical conferences tackling major questions in today's society have also been held with partners such as the University of Leicester, attracting church leaders, Nobel Prize winners and leading politicians. These various pathways—supported by yet others—provide opportunities for people to access 'retreat' at different levels and in different ways. This is important as it has led to many people exploring their sense of spirituality within a secure and trusting environment, who would not otherwise have done so.

This reputation has helped to make Launde self-sustaining as a retreat house and, along with a dedicated and committed staff community, has enabled it to win the Silver Award in the 'Best Tourism Experience 2007–2008' contest for the East Midlands. Interestingly, this award shows how a competitive secular world sees Launde—as somewhere that is accessible for everyone while providing a huge resource to those who come to the Abbey to explore themselves spiritually.

This position is now supported by a redevelopment project which will take Launde into the future. The Stable Block has been enlarged and refurbished to create 19 en-suite bedrooms, due largely to the generosity of the Friends of Launde and individual donations. This will allow Launde to stay open when work is carried out to redevelop the Main House in 2010. All of this work is to further the role of Launde as a retreat house: to be a place of prayer, of peace and of tranquillity in which people can grow spiritually in an increasingly chaotic world.

... exploring their sense of spirituality within a secure and trusting environment

It is vitally important that this work is continued in the future. Launde is ideally placed to do that, but will need the continued prayers and support of all. ∎

More information

To find out more about the work of Launde Abbey and its programme of retreats, please visit www.launde.org.uk or email laundeabbey@leicester.anglican.org

The postal address is Launde Abbey, East Norton, Leicester, LE7 9XB. Telephone: 01572 717254

Noon

These prayers are written by Steve Aisthorpe, recently returned from missionary service in Nepal, where he was Executive Director of the International Nepal Fellowship (INF). He is married to Liz, has two sons, and lives in the Highlands of Scotland.

Many of us begin the day in prayer and scripture reading, seeking to realign ourselves with the Lord and his priorities. But what about at noon? When the sun reaches its zenith and frenzied activity threatens to draw us into a blur of busyness, are we still walking in step with the Spirit?

Sunday

But Jesus often withdrew to lonely places and prayed (Luke 5:16, NIV).

There you were, Lord, the crowds pressing in, multitudes craving your attention, yet you chose to step aside. Your love for each one of the crowd undiminished, you withdrew to spend time with your Father, my Father. I am inspired by the unbroken rhythm of your life: fellowship with the Father and service to people, a constant flow of divine love and power.

Please grant me the wisdom to know when the pace and agenda of this world threaten to interrupt your tempo and divert me from your priorities. Please strengthen my resolve to draw aside to seek your presence and perspective. In those precious moments, please renew my love and equip me for your service. Amen

Monday

The sun stopped shining. And the curtain of the temple was torn in two (Luke 23:45).

Thank you, Lord Jesus, that as darkness descended on that strangest of all noons, you were ready to take upon yourself the sin of the world— and my sin. The vast chasm between God and humanity is bridged; the dividing wall is broken down. I rejoice and praise you for an open door into your presence. You turned the day of evil into the moment of victory.

Please enable me to stand, with my eyes fixed upon you, and see your victories. In the darkest moments may I discern your light and, by your presence and by the joy set before me, be inspired to endure. Amen

Tuesday

Nothing is hidden from its heat (Psalm 19:6).

Lord, you know how it is: by the middle of the day the heat is full on. Sometimes it feels overwhelming; there is no escape, nowhere to hide. Yet where the sun's heat is at its hottest, there its dazzling light is at its most

intense, penetrating in and radiating out.

Lord, in the heat of this day, open my eyes to perceive the light of your presence in each person and in each situation. When there seems to be neither shade nor oasis in sight, grant me the courage to peel back the layers and allow the intense light of your gracious Spirit to search my heart. Please bring growth in all that pleases you within me—and consume all that fights against you. Amen

Wednesday

The Lord is your shade at your right hand (Psalm 121:5).

Heavenly Father, thank you for the assurance of your unfailing protection. In the midst of the day ahead, please screen my vision from being dazzled by the glare of ambition or pride and shield my self-control from being frazzled by the heat. In the challenges of today, please enable me to find rest in the shadow of your almighty presence.

Lord, keeper of Israel, please fulfil your unshakeable promises to all who are especially vulnerable: to those who wrestle with temptation, give strength and a way out; to those in pain and bereavement, bring your comfort; to victims of poverty and injustice, bring relief and hope. Amen

Thursday

The sun stopped in the middle of the sky (Joshua 10:13).

Creator God, sustainer of the universe, everything—all universes, all eternity—is yours. Thank you for the reminder that nothing is impossible for you. Natural and supernatural are one in your eyes; the miraculous is ordinary to you.

Forgive me that I often think and behave as if you are a small god, bound by the norms of this world. Please increase my faith today— enlarge my vision of you. Give me the courage to obey you in all circumstances and the faith to watch out, eagerly and with hope, for you to demonstrate your extravagant love and your awe-inspiring power. Amen

Friday

A furious squall came up, and the waves broke over the boat... Jesus was in the stern, sleeping (Mark 4:37–38).

Lord, I must confess that when the heat is on, I often fear. Like the disciples, in the midst of all kinds of storms I sometimes ask, 'Teacher, don't you care if we drown?'

Please give me the eyes of faith to see you with me—right here, in the same boat. Just as the wind and waves responded to your word, help me, too, in the turmoil of chaos and calamity, to hear and obey your command: 'Quiet! Be still!' God of peace, may I be your agent today, your oil on troubled waters, the bearer of your words to people in fear and hopelessness. Amen

Saturday

Then they called on the name of Baal from morning to noon... Elijah stepped forward and prayed: 'O Lord, God of Abraham, Isaac and Israel, let it be known today that you are God in Israel' (1 Kings 18:26, 36).

Lord God, it was idolatry in broad daylight! Not hidden away in a dark corner but blatant, in the full glare of the sun on top of the highest hill.

Holy God, please give me the sensitivity and determination to discern and uproot the idolatry in my own life—all those things that displace you from the position that is rightfully yours. Lord of my life, please grant me the courage of Elijah. May I, in wisdom, in love and under the guidance of your Holy Spirit, confront idolatry and let it be known in this land that you are God. Amen

Musings of a middle-aged mystic

Veronica Zundel is a journalist, author and contributor to 'New Daylight'. She has also written 'The Time of Our Lives' and 'Crying for the Light' for BRF.

When I started to think about writing this column, from the oldest depths of my memory I dredged up a plaintive, haunting melody—the theme song to the classic film *High Noon*: 'Do not forsake me, oh my darling, on this our wedding day'. In this film, regarded by many as the best Western ever (and reportedly the most requested by US Presidents for showing at the White House), noon is the time of confrontation, when good meets evil for a decisive battle.

I also remember that Andrew Solomon's 'atlas of depression' is entitled *The Noonday Demon*, a reference to Psalm 91:6, which promises protection from 'the destruction that wastes at noonday' (NRSV). Noon is, of course, when the sun is at its fiercest, and in a hot Middle Eastern country its intensity can be unbearable. So noon is the time to down tools for a while, rest in the shade and eat a 'ploughman's lunch' before resuming the hard work of the afternoon. It's a time to take stock, perhaps, of where we have got to and how far there is yet to go along the road.

Noon, then, may be a significant time for a 'middle-aged mystic'. Middle age is, in a sense, the noon of our lives, the halfway point where we assess what we have done with our life so far and ponder what we might do with the rest of it. It may also be a time when we become 'the sandwich generation', squeezed between the demands of growing children and ageing parents. No wonder that's when we are vulnerable to a 'midlife crisis', when we suddenly decide to go blonde or buy a motorbike or, in more drastic cases, leave our partner for a younger or less demanding model.

Being **in the middle** is often an uncomfortable, confusing place to be

Noon is the time of confrontation, when good meets evil for a decisive battle

Should we pay more attention to the noon, or the multiple noons, of our life and what they are saying to us? Noon can be a time to accept that the morning is gone—with its joys, but also with its demands and uncertainties—and to acknowledge that there is still a long haul ahead, with its own tasks but also its own special pleasures and satisfactions.

Being 'in the middle' is often an uncomfortable, confusing place to be.

As a single woman at an age when most of my contemporaries were married, I used to compare my situation to someone who had begun to cross a road but only got as far as the halfway island. I couldn't go back to being identified mainly as my parents' daughter, but neither could I go forward to become someone's partner. I had to find my identity alone, and it was an unsettling place to be in. (Of course, when I finally did get married, there was a whole new set of problems to negotiate!)

Theologian Richard Rohr talks about the two halves of life. In the first half, our task is to create our external identity, to 'prove ourselves' through work, through relationships, through creativity. In the second, it is time to let go of all we have built up and instead to nurture our internal life, our spiritual being. Rohr also claims that the only reliable way of moving someone who has got 'stuck' in the first half on to the second half is by some form of suffering. As someone for whom middle age coincided with a breakdown and a child with a disability, I find a lot of truth in his analysis.

At noon on Good Friday, as Jesus hung on the cross and cried his last, forsaken cry, darkness descended on the whole land. If the brightness of noon sometimes feels like darkness to you, may you find light as you face the afternoon. ■

Do take a moment to visit the *Quiet Spaces* website (www.quietspaces.org.uk) and email us with your thoughts, perhaps sparked by what you have read in this issue.

In our next issue

Night—shadows lengthening and the moon rising above the rooftops; the coming of 'star-less and Bible black' darkness; the long sleep which may be troubled or consoled by dreams; the dark night of the soul endured by those feeling cut off from God's presence.

In the final issue of *Quiet Spaces* for 2008, we ponder night—for some a step into the unknown, a time they face with anxiety; for others the chance for rest and peace after long labours.

Contact us at:

Quiet Spaces,
BRF,
15 The Chambers,
Vineyard, Abingdon
OX14 3FE
enquiries@brf.org.uk

QUIET SPACES SUBSCRIPTIONS

Quiet Spaces is published three times a year, in March, July and November. To take out a subscription, please complete this form, indicating the month in which you would like your subscription to begin.

☐ I would like to give a gift subscription (please complete both name and address sections below)

☐ I would like to take out a subscription myself (complete name and address details only once)

This completed coupon should be sent with appropriate payment to BRF. Alternatively, please write to us quoting your name, address, the subscription you would like for either yourself or a friend (with their name and address), the start date and credit card number, expiry date and signature if paying by credit card.

Gift subscription name _____

Gift subscription address _____

_____

_____ Postcode _____

Please send beginning with the next July / November / March issue: *(delete as applicable)*

(please tick box)	UK	SURFACE	AIR MAIL
Quiet Spaces	☐ £16.95	☐ £18.45	☐ £20.85

Please complete the payment details below and send your coupon, with appropriate payment to: BRF, 15 The Chambers, Vineyard, Abingdon OX14 3FE.

Name _____

Address _____

Postcode _____ Telephone Number _____

Email _____

☐ Please do not email me any information about BRF publications

Method of payment: ☐ Cheque ☐ Mastercard ☐ Visa ☐ Maestro ☐ Postal Order

Card no. ☐☐☐☐ ☐☐☐☐ ☐☐☐☐ ☐☐☐☐ ☐☐☐☐

Valid from ☐☐☐☐ Expires ☐☐☐☐ Issue no. of Maestro card ☐☐☐

Security Code ☐☐☐

Signature _____ Date ___ / ___ / _____

All orders must be accompanied by the appropriate payment.
Please make cheques payable to BRF

☐ Please do not send me further information about BRF publications

PROMO REF: QSNOON

BRF is a Registered Charity

64